LOVE TOO CAN
SPREAD

Enjoy the book!

Ali Satoh

LOVE TOO
CAN SPREAD

POETRY FROM THE MIDST OF A PANDEMIC

ARI SATOK

Love Too Can Spread:
Poetry From the Midst of a Pandemic
1st Edition

ISBN: 978-0-9978435-2-1

For more information about the author, visit *www.arisatok.com*

Dedication

To all those who lost their lives to the coronavirus, and to the brave doctors and nurses who've worked tirelessly on behalf of us all.

LOVE TOO CAN SPREAD

It is possible, I believe,
To hold heaviness lightly
To be calmly afraid
To cling to shreds of the ordinary
Even in the most abnormal of times

Fear cannot be quarantined
But neither can love,
Love too can spread,
Catastrophe can hold in it the seeds of compassion
If we choose to let them grow.

Contents

Introduction

LIKE EVERYONE ELSE on this planet, my world changed completely in 2020.

Maybe I shouldn't have been so surprised, since the pandemic – which would leave almost nothing the same as it had been before – had already been upending the world before I took notice. First in China. Then in Iran. Italy. Spain.

We'd seen news of it in our newspapers in New York City, watched it on our TV screens. And yet, somehow, we did not believe that it could happen to us too. Tragedy often seems light-years away until it has fully arrived.

Now the coronavirus had arrived and now New York City was its global epicenter. Now the theaters and the restaurants and the museums that gave this city its vibrancy had shut their doors, and now, the lives we inhabited looked nothing like the ones that had been ours just days before.

One moment, we were riding the subways wherever and whenever we pleased; we were celebrating birthdays in overflowing apartments; we were standing shoulder to shoulder in Starbucks to get our morning coffees. And then the next moment – or at least that's how it felt – we were sheltered at home, save for the brave essential workers staffing our hospitals, stocking our supermarkets, and keeping our city alive.

One moment, we were planning all sorts of adventures: buying concert tickets, booking trips, arranging weddings. And then the next, it was as if geography and time had collapsed. Suddenly, we were going nowhere other than where we already were, and the future – that place of possibility in which we tend to store so much of ourselves – was far too foggy to plan for at all. It's wild how quickly everything can change.

INTRODUCTION

I remember the week when you could suddenly feel that change everywhere. It was a week filled with panic shopping, as more and more of the world announced its temporary closure. Universities moved online. The NBA declared a pause on its season. The Met closed. MoMA. Carnegie Hall. Even Broadway turned off its lights. But despite the panic, I still believed that this new pandemic reality would disappear as quickly as it had come.

At the end of that week, I was staying with my girlfriend at my apartment on the Upper West Side of Manhattan. I can still remember the day, March 15, when we left my apartment and headed to hers in Brooklyn.

I packed a small suitcase with enough clothes for about five days, leaving behind a large stack of library books and a bedroom floor covered in grocery bags filled with non-perishable foods I'd bought in the week prior; I assumed I'd be back in a week.

It would be three full months until I returned. When my girlfriend and I finally felt safe enough to take an Uber and cross back into Manhattan, my room was waiting just as I'd left it. The pile of books and the grocery bags on the floor and the unmade bed were exactly as they'd been before. But by then, the entire world outside my window was completely and wholly transformed. It's wild how quickly everything can change.

* * *

Those initial months of the pandemic – and the many months since – have been unusual. Bewildering. Often surreal. In early March 2020, the idea of New York City streets with shuttered stores and masked people would have seemed like science fiction; by the end of March, it was reality.

INTRODUCTION

More than a year later, we are still the same people we were at the beginning of that first pandemic March. And yet – we're not. For, in the blink of an eye, all of the certainties with which we walked through the world crumbled completely. Over and over again, when I video chat with friends and family, we drift into moments of shared disbelief. It's wild how quickly everything can change.

* * *

When the world changes, it's inevitable that we change along with it. When certainty shatters and all of the well-worn tracks we've always traveled disappear, we – by necessity – find new ways to live. We've had birthday parties on Zoom. We've clapped for our first responders so they can hear our love even when they can't see us. We've reimagined how we teach and learn, how we pray and gather.

So much of this change has been difficult and sometimes even disheartening – chaos has the capacity to bring out new ugliness, to give selfishness new form. But what has struck me in these tumultuous, uncertain times, is how many people have responded with goodness – with an urge to help their neighbors in whatever ways they can.

As the pandemic pulled back the curtains that hide our vulnerability, it seems to me that we've realized more than ever how intertwined we all are. We've located in ourselves reserves of resilience we may not have thought we had, and we've discovered, perhaps most importantly of all, our capacity to make a difference in the lives of others. To be, in the stunning words of Maya Angelou, "the rainbow in someone else's cloud."

* * *

INTRODUCTION

Mr. Rogers, the famous children's television personality, said, "When I was a boy and I would see scary things in the news, my mother would say to me, 'Look for the helpers. You will always find people who are helping.'"

The helpers in this pandemic have been all around us – people of all ages and all backgrounds, taking their abilities and their resources and using them to benefit others.

There have been the obvious helpers – the brave doctors and nurses, the food bank operators, the politicians who have chosen to put the greater good over politics. The shelf stockers who have kept our grocery stores stocked, the postal workers who have kept our mail arriving, the transit workers who have kept our subways and buses operational.

But the "helpers" in this moment haven't only been our essential workers, to whom we owe an enormous debt. The helpers have been all of us: the daughter who grocery shopped for her aging mom, the father who stayed up extra late to help his son with his homework, the granddaughter who called her grandpa every night just to say, "I love you."

The helpers have been the ones carrying out the grand gestures – fundraising millions of dollars, livestreaming their concerts and comedy shows into the living rooms of thousands – but the helpers have just as much been the ones easing the burden of other people's lives in quiet, compassionate, completely unheralded ways.

In this pandemic moment, it has sometimes seemed to me that each of us has been dropping whatever little somethings we can offer into the bucket of love our world so desperately needs in order to heal. And perhaps together – I've continued to hope – we can fill that bucket up.

One of my little drops in the bucket has been my poetry. When the pandemic started, like so many people, I tried to think about what I could possibly do or offer to alleviate some of the suffering and difficulty that was overwhelming the world. As a young poet, the answer felt clear to me. I could give my words. Try my best to make them beautiful and comforting and sometimes light and funny, and share them with people in the hope that occasionally words – well-chosen and well-arranged – could make someone feel a little bit better. And so, each week of this pandemic, I sent out a poem to hundreds of people – hoping my words would make my readers smile, or laugh, or feel comforted and less alone in very lonely times.

* * *

There's a fair question that can be asked in moments of crisis. Does art, poetry included, really matter? Medicine obviously matters. Personal protective equipment and ventilators and testing kits matter. But does art?

I think the answer this pandemic has given us is clear. That art does matter – that it too, in a way different from medicine and a meal to eat and a roof over our heads – is essential. We need art to process catastrophe as we live through it. And we need art as well, I would argue, to ultimately heal. We need music and movies, novels and TV shows, paintings and plays. And we need poems too.

I've encountered that need in the myriad beautiful responses I've received from the recipients of my weekly poems. When the situation in Italy was at its worst, I got an email from a couple in Rome expressing their appreciation for a poem of mine, who wrote, "Its truthfulness and encouragement pierces through our veil of anxiety." In response to another poem that I sent, a friend offered perhaps the best compliment a poet could receive: "I needed your poem today."

Poems, much like good hugs, can sometimes make us feel safe and cozy and warm inside. They can inspire us, make us laugh, and draw our attention places it never otherwise would have wandered. They can give us a new lens to see old things, or an old lens to see new ones. They can challenge the status quo and conjure visions of new futures for the world to strive for. In this book are poems that aim to do all of those things – poems that I very much hope will find homes in the hearts of those who read them.

* * *

Many poetry collections are consistent in their tone. This collection is deliberately not. Some poems are deeply serious, while others are lighthearted and humorous. The somber and the upbeat, the disappointed and the hopeful, exist together.

I've chosen to include in this book poems with such varied tones because it feels reflective of the lived experience of the pandemic months when I wrote it. So many different emotions and feelings were being experienced side-by-side, and I wanted the book to mirror that. When I feel it's necessary, I contextualize certain poems, and I've included some short paragraphs between poems that I think help weave this book together.

* * *

It's strange to write a book with no clue at all of what kind of world it will be published into. Will we still be largely in our homes? Will vaccination be widespread? Will we be more compassionate or more corrupt? Will the virus have mutated further? Will things look much the same as they did before this pandemic, or will our world be getting reimagined in dramatic ways each and every day? We do not know. All we know is that it will continue to be our choice whether or not to learn the lessons, personal and collective, that this moment we are experiencing can teach us.

In early May 2020, I was facilitating a writing workshop over the phone for a group of senior citizens and I asked them explicitly what lessons they felt they'd learned so far from the pandemic. Before the pandemic, I'd met with this group in person every week, but now the phone was our only way of connecting and so I sat in Brooklyn, as the seniors, mostly in their 70s and 80s, sat alone, isolated in their apartments in Manhattan. One by one, their voices came through the phone, answering my question.

Arlene had learned to find time for things she'd never made time for before. Harry had discovered new ways to connect with the people and communities that were dear to him. Morrie had learned that he communicated better through hugs than words, and that he missed human touch more than anything else. No two answers were the same.

In the weeks, and months, and years to come, all of us will continue to search for our own answers as to the question of what lessons we've drawn from this ongoing moment. This book is my best answer right now. I hope it helps you find yours.

"Everything can change in an instant. Everything. And then there is only before and after."

Phyllis Reynolds Naylor

When Everything Changed

I just checked the New York Times again
For the fourteenth time this hour.

I watch the numbers rise and rise,
Watch the experts offer up their wisdom
And the pundits offer up their anger;
The world is a sometimes-scary place.

A week ago
I went to Trader Joe's
To buy some groceries
And the lineup weaved its way through an entire floor of
the store.

I asked the cashier if people were stockpiling food,
He laughed
And said he'd just rung up a woman
Buying thirty cans of garbanzo beans.

I laughed too,
For laughter is often the strongest weapon
With which to fight fear,
But it was the kind of laugh
That wasn't fully sure
Of its own appropriateness;
The world is a sometimes-scary place.

The cashier gave me my bags
And I exited the store
Returning to streets
Where people tried to go about their lives as usual when
nothing was as usual,
Their phones pinging with the anxieties and the love of
family members miles away.

WHEN EVERYTHING CHANGED

Here was a city, like so many others,
Trying to learn
How to juggle caution and normalcy,
How to heed what needs to be heeded,
How to meet the world
One day at a time.

Here was a city,
Stumbling in the dark,
Searching for safe haven
In the face of a raging storm.

Some storms pass quickly and leave very little imprint in their wake. This storm, alas, was not one of those.

This storm came and then it did not quickly disappear. Instead, it spread and it grew, tearing down so much of the invisible architecture of our lives. Whatever scripts had guided us through life before suddenly seemed irrelevant.

Unprecedented days awaited us. And we had no choice but to figure out how to live them.

The Ways We Filled Our Lives

When the invisible architecture of our lives came tumbling down
What did we do?

We social distanced.
We grocery shopped.
We cooked.
We dreamed.
We called our grandparents and told them that we loved them.
We lazed.
We cried.
We walked.
We made big deals out of small things.
We made small deals out of big things.
We worked.
We pretended to work.
We snacked
We matured.
We regressed.
We Zoomed.
We moped.
We read.
We grieved.
We fought.
We made up.
We fought again.
We clung to hope.
We lost hope.
We were patient.
We were impatient.
We expressed our thanks.
We gave kindness.
We received kindness.
We grew out our hair.
We lost track of time.
We noticed things we'd never noticed before.
We felt things we'd never felt before.

THE WAYS WE FILLED OUR LIVES

When the invisible architecture of our lives disappeared
We found new ways to live.

Sometimes creatively,
Sometimes compassionately,
Sometimes in joy and sometimes in sadness,
Sometimes in gratitude and sometimes in longing,
Sometimes with grace and sometimes with anything but.

There were days on which we wanted nothing more than our
old lives back.
But there were days too, on which we found beauty in our new,
strange ones–
Days on which we managed to live and love and learn,
Even as the whole world turned
In ways it had never turned before in our lives.

We Social ⊢——6 FT——⊣ Distanced.

Goodbye for Now to the Days Before

Goodbye for now to the days before
Of concerts and parties and crowded trains,
Of UberPool and happy hour,
Of sitting in middle seats on planes.

Goodbye for now to the days before
Of theater and cruises and hotel buffets,
Of coffee dates and water parks,
Of long, unhurried museum days.

Goodbye for now to the days before
Of pub crawls and galas and county fairs,
Of casino nights and carefree hugs,
Of dinners with friends and communal prayers.

Goodbye for now to the days before
Of family trips and office routine;
Hello for now to these homebound days,
To the start of life in quarantine.

I vividly remember the strangeness of those early days in lockdown, texting with friends and family as we tried to collectively make sense of our new reality. I remember the confusion and the fear and the uncertainty.

At the beginning of March 2020, the phrase "social distancing" hadn't even been in our vocabularies. By the end of March, it was all we were talking about.

We were worrying about the loneliness and isolation social distancing was already causing and we were wondering when we would next be able to step foot in a theater or a restaurant or a school.

In the midst of this collective worry, I decided to write a poem that I hoped could offer just a little bit of a different framing on what were sure to be difficult times ahead.

There were so many wonderful people in each of our lives we temporarily would not get to see in-person. But what if – I wondered with a laugh – for just a brief moment, we focused instead on the less wonderful ones we would temporarily get to avoid?

The Upside of Social Distancing

Even when this all is over
And corona fades away
I still plan to social distance
From my downer cousin Ray,

And I'm going to skip all happy hours
With my neurotic colleague Jill,
And I'm done with getting coffee
With my judgy roommate Bill,

And I'll keep six feet of distance
From my boastful uncle Ross,
Even more if I am able
From my overbearing boss,

And I'll cut off all engagements
With my high school buddy Dwight,
Who is somehow almost always wrong
Yet thinks he's always right,

And I'm finished with all dinners
With Miguel, my oldest friend,
For he talks but never listens
And his stories never end................

It is hard to have to distance
From the friends I've long enjoyed,
But it's made a whole lot easier
When I focus on those I'll avoid.

We Shopped For Groceries.

In our new socially distanced lives, my girlfriend and I barely left her apartment. Once or twice a day, we'd go outside for a short walk. Very occasionally, we'd pick something up at a corner store or pharmacy. And so it was only a matter of time until our supermarket excursions – once every couple of weeks – became the central drama of our quarantined lives.

Prepping for a Pandemic

Stock up on beans, the experts say,
And lentils could be nice,
Peas in a can and frozen fish
And noodles and tuna and rice.

I won't deny, that's good advice
For storage and budget's sake,
But the experts clearly forgot one thing–
Stock up on chocolate cake!

The Wondrous Variety of Grocery Store Purchases

My neighbor bought some truffles
And some gnocchi and some kale,
A little bit of saffron
And a lot of yellowtail,

Some walnuts and some goat cheese
And a bag of Terra Chips,
Some farro and some olives
And three types of fancy dips,

Some cumin and some nutmeg,
And a bottle of Chardonnay,
Plus everything he's going to need
To make a cheese soufflé.

* * *

I bought Eggo waffles
And three bags of Milky Ways,
Some Oreos, some M&Ms,
And donuts topped with glaze,

Some Twizzlers and some Gushers
And a box of Cap'n Crunch,
A little bit of pasta
And some Lunchables for lunch.

* * *

My girlfriend says my palate
Is a little unrefined;
I prefer to use the term
"Deliciously-inclined."

Oh the Way You Now Shop

This poem is modeled after one of the iconic parts of Dr. Seuss's magnificent book *Oh the Places You'll Go.*

> You have gloves on your hands,
> And a mask on your face,
> You are fully surrounded by six feet of space.
>
> You know where to go
> For you've done this before,
> You're a champion here in this grocery store.

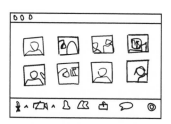

We Zoomed.

When the pandemic started, I'm not certain I even had a Zoom account. By the end of March, the line between life and life on Zoom was beginning to grow increasingly blurry.

My Changed Life

My life was once a range of things,
Movies, concerts, Tinder flings,
Bars with way too little room;
Now it's only calls on Zoom.

Big Group Call

Eight little faces in eight little squares
Nobody knows who should talk;
I think it's time to get off this call
And go and take a walk.

Math Class on Zoom

My teacher thinks I'm listening,
If truth be told, I'm not;
But I don't think she'd be mad at me
If she saw the pants I just bought!

Grandma and Her Webcam

Grandma seems to like to Zoom
And tell me how she's feeling;
I just wish that her webcam
Wasn't pointed at the ceiling.

How To Leave a Zoom Call

Conversation starts to wane,
"It's hard to hear," you shout,
And then you say the magic words:
"I think I'm cutting out."

We Checked The News.
Again. And Again.

Like most people, I sometimes found Zoom exhausting. But it wasn't only Zoom that was tiring me out. Equally exhausting was the news, with its steady stream of terrifying headlines.

I'm not sure what I was really looking for every time I checked the news in those first months of the pandemic. Was it hope? Confirmation of the worst? An article that could magically tell me precisely when "normal" would return?

* * *

It was during the pandemic that I encountered a word that so perfectly summed up a behavioral trap I would often fall into: doomscrolling. It was like my thumb couldn't stop itself, scrolling endlessly through news feeds and news sites that offered nothing but a never-ending onslaught of terribly distressing news.

I Checked the News at 10 AM

I checked the news at 10 a.m.
And then at 10:04,
And then at just past 10:09
I checked the news some more,

And then I checked at 10:16
And then at 10:18,
10:20 and 10:29
And six times in between.

I'm not sure why I check so much
Since it only brings distress;
Maybe I should try to check
The news a little less.

Find Me a Channel

Find me a channel with only good news,
With livestreams of pandas and cute kangaroos,
And shows about grandmothers playing kazoos,
And lumberjack children who sing in canoes,
And baritone Brits reading movie reviews.

Find me a channel with only good news;
And if you can't find one, then find me some booze.

Old Uncle Bob

They always judged old Uncle Bob
For his choice to live under a rock;
So when he returned to the world last week
His family was in shock.

He asked for the news from the year he'd been gone
For he did not have even a clue;
They told him of fires in the Australian bush
And of ones in the Amazon, too.

They told him of Kobe Bryant's death
And that migrants were being detained,
And they said that a virus was spreading fast
With no sign yet of being contained.

"I see," said Bob, with an aching heart,
"This news is so heavy to bear,
I think I'll return to live under my rock
For it's much more pleasant there."

We Washed Our Hands.
Again. And Again.

I can still remember the shortage of hand sanitizer in the earliest days of the pandemic. Like with toilet paper and masks, demand simply exceeded supply. But despite the shortage, every so often I would find in a grocery store or pharmacy a little bit of stock, a few bottles perhaps of a product I'd never paid much attention to before that was suddenly as precious as gold.

The Purell Brigade

Here we stand on this Walmart shelf,
My fellow Purells and I,
Ready to meet this moment
And take up the battle cry.

Here we wait to serve with pride
From the moment that we're bought,
Ready to do our humble parts
In this war that must be fought.

Here we share heartfelt goodbyes
Before we all disperse,
Ready for our deployments
To the bottom of every purse.

We'll give until there's nothing left
We're fierce and unafraid;
We are the brave, the strong, the few
The mighty Purell Brigade.

Handwashing Olympics

If they held an Olympics for washing hands
I think I'd win the gold;
They say the way I scrub my nails
Is a marvel to behold.

They say the way I take my time
Is the apex of technique;
They say the way I lather
Is incredibly unique.

And they say I'm at my best now,
All this extra training helps;
If they held an Olympics for washing hands
I'd be the Michael Phelps.

Rest in Peace Mr. Handshake

As hand washing increased exponentially, handshaking quickly became a thing of the past.

* * *

Rest in peace Mr. Handshake
You lived a wondrous life;
We share this grief with your children
And your grieving, gracious wife.

You were there for generations
From antiquity till now;
You were firmer than the fist bump
You were warmer than the bow.

You were solid, you were trusting,
You were confident and strong;
Rest in peace Mr. Handshake
It's sad to say "So long!"

We Wore Masks.

By April 2020, our coronavirus precautions in New York City included not only handwashing but also mask-wearing. I wore them everywhere outside of my girlfriend's apartment – even on walks outside. Sometimes, I'd imagine my favorite mask-wearing fictional characters, and wonder what they would have thought of our newly masked-up world.

Maskwearers Anonymous

This support group was convened in the third week of widespread mask-wearing. Here is a transcript of the beginning of the first session.

* * *

Support Group Leader:

"Welcome to this support group
It's brave of you all to come;
We're here to help each other deal
With the things we're hurting from.

I wish we were in person
But we'll make the best of Zoom;
And a reminder: nothing said tonight
Is allowed to leave this "room."

So let's start with introductions,
Your name and where you are;
Then tell us how you're doing
In this time that's so bizarre."

Batman

"I'm Batman, I'm in Gotham
I've been sheltering in my cave –
With Robin, Robin's mother,
And a college friend named Dave,

And I'm kind of embarrassed to say it aloud
For it feels quite immature,
But to live in a world where everyone's masked
Makes me somewhat insecure.

Let's be clear – I'm very grateful
All my neighbors wear a mask;
It's the time now, more than ever,
To do what the experts ask.

All these rules are for good reason,
Which is why we must comply;
It's just hard to have once been "the man with the mask"
When I'm now just a regular guy."

Spiderman

"I'm Spiderman, in NYC,
At my aunt's place out in Queens;
It's been an awful half-a-year
But I'm finding some new routines.

I've been making lots of sourdough
And getting through Game of Thrones,
Plus I've started doing yoga
To deal with the world's unknowns.

And I'm here in this support group
Since I've been feeling somewhat down,
For I used to be recognized all the time
Wherever I'd walk around,

But now that the city's wearing masks
I'm noticed so much less,
And though I wish I could shrug it off
It's causing me some distress.

Yes – I know my mask's still different
Since it covers the whole of my face;
But I'm feeling less special than I did before
In this fully masked-up place."

Phantom of the Opera

"I'm the Phantom of the Opera,
I'm in Paris, on my own;
It's been tougher than expected
Quarantining all alone,

For although I was a recluse
Well before corona hit,
Even recluses get lonely
Sometimes more than they admit.

All the news has sapped my focus
So I can't compose or write;
It's been weeks since I've made progress
On The Music of the Night

And like Spiderman and Batman
My biggest fear this week,
Is that now that the whole world's wearing masks
I'm no longer unique."

Support Group Leader:

"It makes sense to feel these feelings
This new world is very strange,
And for almost everyone I know
It's hard to deal with change.

So today we'll start discussing
How to cope with what we feel;
I will do my best to share some tools
That I think can help you heal.

But let's finish introductions first
So we know each other's names,
And if we have time at the very end
We can play a couple games.

Ooooo…. I'm seeing a new arrival
Who's just popped up on this call;
Mr. Vader, please unmute yourself
We can't hear you yet at all.

Tell us where you are and why you're here
Then Zorro, it's your turn;
And remember friends, no judging here
Just listen, love and learn."

In our newly masked lives, I usually wore a standard blue disposable mask. But every so often, when I felt like I needed extra protection for a particular errand I was running, I turned to the gold standard of masks: the N95.

Tales of an N95

"When I was a wee-little N95
I always felt somewhat uncool,
For I felt like a far less pretty mask
Than the rest of the masks at my school.

There were Broadway masks in my homeroom class
Who seemed confident as could be;
Yet no matter how nice I was to them
They never noticed me.

There were Mardi Gras masks with feathers and glitz
That were flashy and splashy and grand,
There were Halloween masks in my after school club
Who would say that they thought I was bland.

* * *

Well I'm suddenly, in these scary times,
The most popular mask of all;
And I think of the many years I've lived
When I often was made to feel small,

And I think of the work that I'm doing now
Helping doctors keep patients alive;
And I think of how honored I feel today
In my job as an N95,

And I think of one thing that my father said
When I'd come home from school feeling glum;
He would say to me: "You're beautiful
And I promise your time will come."

We Netflixed A lot.

For the rare moments when I wasn't mask-wearing, handwashing, Zooming or relentlessly checking the news, I – like everyone else – had to find new leisure activities to occupy my time.

I remember the ambition of my aspirations in the early months of the pandemic. I imagined that I'd listen to lectures, invent new games, learn a language, even pick up the ukulele. Those aspirations proved overly ambitious. But I certainly succeeded in one thing: watching more Netflix than I ever had before.

The Boy Who Could Not Stop Watching

Have you heard the strange and peculiar tale
Of Emmanuel Hugo Von Crouch?
They say that for all of quarantine
He never left his couch.

They say from the moment he woke each day
He turned his Netflix on,
And watched till the moment he went to bed,
Then started again at dawn.

They say his parents begged him
To at least take a little break;
To go outside or read a book,
For theirs – if not his – sake.

But they say he wouldn't leave the couch
It was like it was made of glue;
And though it caused his parents grief
There was nothing that they could do.

And they say that the scariest thing of all
Is not how long it's been;
But that now you can't tell where Emmanuel ends
And where the couch begins.

Quarantine Goals Versus Reality

I thought I would write a movie script
And read three books a week;
I thought I'd do yoga every night
And work on my cooking technique,

I thought I would keep a daily blog
And learn to play guitar;
I thought I would pick up Japanese
And become a YouTube star,

I thought I would either learn to knit
Or learn to quilt instead;
And like everyone else on my Instagram feed
I thought I would learn to bake bread.

But what have I done, oh what have I done
In this quarantined start of spring?
I've mostly napped and snacked and slept
And binge-watched Tiger King.

What Shall We Watch Tonight?

Maybe something funny…
Like American Pie
Or Family Guy
Or I guess we could try Stranger Things?
Lord of the Rings?
Or how 'bout watching the start of Veep?
Or anything with Meryl Streep?
Or I could go for School of Rock?
Or an early film of Ethan Hawke?

Or what do you think of the Wizard of Oz?
Or something thrilling – maybe Jaws?
Or a war film – maybe Black Hawk Down?
Or something British – like The Crown?
Or a Marvel movie – maybe Thor?
Or a Harry Potter – maybe 4?
Or Parasite, or La La Land?
Or the newest Alice In Wonderland?
Or I'd even go for Frozen 2….

Not one of these sounds good to you??

Is there anything that you'd propose?
No… I'm not into cooking shows…
No… I'm not in the mood for Crash….
Another time we'll try out M*A*S*H

1 hour later. Still no choice.

You're scared to try the Walking Dead?
You know what – let's just go to bed.

We Lost Track Of Time.

In the Netflix and anxiety-filled early months of the pandemic, it became very easy to lose track of time. First, it was the days blurring into each other, then the weeks, then even the months.

At the beginning of May, I got an email that ended with the line "Have a great weekend (whatever that means these days)." It made me laugh.

Time had once been so demarcated: work days separated from vacation days, mornings and afternoons out separated from evenings at home, hours spent in community separated from hours spent alone. Now time was so much more undifferentiated – like a vast plain stretching forward with nothing at all out on the horizon.

Saturday Goes to Therapy

This poem is imagined in the voice of Saturday, grappling
with how the pandemic impacts his status in relation to his six
brothers, the other six days of the week.

* * *

I grew up the sixth of seven
And my childhood was heaven
For before this virus struck it felt so clear

I was everyone's favorite child
When they saw me, people smiled
They would always say "Yay! Saturday is here!"

I was different than my brothers
More beloved than the others
Even Sunday wasn't quite as liked as me;

I was respite from the hustle
Of my weekday brothers' bustle,
I was sleep-ins, I was Sabbath, I was free.

Now I get mixed up with Monday
Who's the farthest from a fun day
With his anxious vibes of going back to work;

Someone thought that I was Tuesday
Do I seem like such a snooze day?
All this new confusion's driving me berserk.

I'm less special, I'm less savored,
And I'm certainly less favored
In the days since cases first began to spike;

It is even hard for Mother
To discern me from my brothers
For she claims this virus makes us look alike.

Landscapes in Time

I remember when time
Had as many topographies
As the marvelous Earth on which we walk.

There were moments that felt as constricted
As a narrow gorge,
Moments as scary as a lightless cave,
Moments as vast as the Serengeti,
As comforting as the ocean,
As transcendent as the Grand Canyon.

Now the moments all feel alike to me,
Now I wait,
To return to landscapes in time,
That I have not visited for months.
Now I wait,
For yesterday to finally find its place in the past,
And for tomorrow to gleam with hope again,
Re-learning how to welcome the world,
Into the magnificence
Of its endless possibility.

Despite the loss of so many of our normal markers of time, there were still three things that kept me at least somewhat tethered to time.

First, there were the holidays. Though I celebrated them in markedly different ways than ever before, the pandemic could not make them fully disappear. Passover, even without an overflowing table of aunts and uncles and cousins to share it with, was still Passover.

Second, there were the seasons. With so many of the manmade markers of time gone, I found myself noticing the natural ones more than I ever had before. The changes in the weather. The blooming of flowers in the spring. The falling of leaves in the autumn. The hot summer nights. The 5 p.m. darkness in the winter. Nature had always kept time for us; but it was only now, it seemed, that I was fully paying attention.

And third, there was my rapidly growing hair, longer and longer each time I looked in the bathroom mirror.

With barbershops closed, the world was filling up with newly longhaired men like me. The shaggier we all got, the clearer it became that the pandemic was going to last for a very long time.

The Delight of an Amateur Barber

My dream came true this morning,
I feel like I'm walking on air!
I got the opportunity
To cut my brother's hair!

He asked for a normal haircut
"Of course," is what I said;
But I hope he's fine, that I changed my mind
And gave him a mullet instead.

We Went Stir Crazy.

As my hair grew even longer and my hopes for a quick return to pre-pandemic normal continued to shrink, I started to encounter in my conversations with friends and family a growing sense that more and more people were feeling positively stir-crazy.

To combat the increasing sense of cabin fever, once in a while I'd talk with someone about where we hoped to travel when everything one day got back to normal. It was a way for us to, at least mentally, swap out our scenery. If in reality we couldn't go anywhere much beyond the front doors of our apartments, at the very least we could imagine and dream.

To Travel in the Mind

When my mind is feeling lost and scared
In the fog of a heartbreaking day,
I close my weary eyes sometimes
And imagine I'm far away,

And I drift to the hills of Tuscany
In the gentle, evening light,
And I glide through the fjords of Norway
On a perfect starry night,

And I stand in the Himalayas
As if floating in the clouds,
And I lie on the sands in Fiji
Far away from the city's crowds,

And I walk through the redwood forests
As the birds fly overhead,
And I roam in an alpine meadow
Where the flowers of spring have spread,

And I sit by the Seine in Paris
By the light of a crescent moon,
And I trek through the Gobi Desert
Past the base of a great sand dune,

And when finally I awaken
And I watch today unfold,
I somehow find this heavy world
Feels easier to hold.

Take Me to the Taj Mahal

Take me to the Taj Mahal,
To the Palace of Versailles,
To the Grand Canal of Venice,
To the towers of Dubai,

To the pyramids of Giza,
To the Pantheon in Rome;
Honestly – just take me
Any place that's not my home.

Oh How the Times Have Changed

I used to go to Burning Man,
And Justin Bieber shows;
I'd dine with Lady Gaga,
And jam with Axl Rose

I'd never miss the Oscars
Nor galas at the Met;
I'd party out in Vegas
And win big at roulette

I'd join the Times Square ball drop
With childlike delight;
And when a good play opened
I'd be at opening night

But now, in these more homebound times,
In truth, I must confess:
By far, my most exciting plans
Are trips to CVS.

Pandemic Migration

"It's time for migration," said the mother bird,
"We're leaving New York today,
Go say goodbye to your Central Park friends
Then we're off and on our way."

"Are we going back to Rio?"
Asked the youngest daughter Screech,
"I love it there, with its samba shows,
And the Copacabana Beach."

"I wish that we could," said the mother bird
"I love it too my dear,"
"But their Covid numbers are still too high
So we can't go back this year."

"Are we going to Miami?"
Asked the eldest daughter Squeak,
"The nightlife there's amazing
And the boardwalk's really chic."

"I wish that we could," said the mother bird
"But that trip will have to wait
For Covid hit Florida very hard
And it's rising again in the state."

"Are we going to Bermuda?"
Asked the middle daughter Beak,
"Or to Malta or Tahiti?
Or Peru or Martinique?"

"I wish that we could," said the mother bird
"We've got cousins in Peru,
But alas with this virus as bad as it is,
We are going somewhere new.

WE WENT STIR CRAZY

To a land far-away from this city,
That they say is a magical place;
Where a bird can fly any which way that she wants
With no fear and no mask on her face,

To a land where they say there are Hobbits,
Where the mountains watch over the sea,
Where they say that the people are lovely
And that healthcare is practically free,

Where the virus has fully been vanquished,
What a distant hope that seems;
We are off to a land called New Zealand
The land of the whole world's dreams."

We Enjoyed The Outdoors.

With no ability to travel anywhere, I – like so many others – learned to at least find joy in the short little walks I'd take near my apartment. Simply being outdoors became an enormous source of comfort.

Quarantine, by its nature, made the world feel small; going outside was a way of restoring a sense of vastness.

Just looking at the sky, the moon, and the sun could transport me – even if only briefly– outside of the devastating realities the pandemic was foisting upon humanity.

It was a way of remembering that though the world's problems were large, the world itself was larger. It was a way of remembering that all things, even the worst of them, would one day pass and eventually be nothing more than a small ripple in the infinite ocean of time.

Canopied by the Sky

I never used to think of it as a gift to myself
To shed walls and windows
For fresher air,
To be canopied by sky
And kissed by the sun,
But now I do –
Now it is often more precious than anything else,
The feeling of vastness,
When the world feels most constrained.

So many of our greatest gifts
Never announce themselves as such
And so we sometimes miss the magic held within them.

Not long ago, I often sped from my apartment to the subway.

There was so much to be late for then
If I did not move fast enough,
Or so I thought,
And so I raced to the places I thought I needed to be,
Missing the sky,
And the trees,
And the cherry blossoms,
And all the other little ways the world,
Even amidst racing streets
And crowded sidewalks
Still glows with beauty.

Now I am always on time,
Now I must be nowhere but where I am,
Now I walk slowly,
And see the flowers,
And the dancing light,
And the setting sun,
Now there is nowhere left to run
And so I am here,
Perhaps where I was always meant to be.

New Hobbies

My buddy Ken was never into hikes,
But he went last month and posted and he got a lot of likes,
And I think he liked the likes a lot, so he chose to hike again,
Now he goes so often that we call him Hiker Ken.

* * *

My classmate Hayley never liked to bike,
But she bought one when she read online that sales began to spike;
She claimed to want to "try" a sport that one could do alone
I think she just can't stand not having things that others own.

* * *

My neighbor Candace never liked to run,
But she did like posting selfies at the moment she was done;
She's gotten to the point now where she posts one every day,
I think it's time that from her posts I start to stay away.

* * *

My colleague Sarah never liked to swim,
But she's started since her building had to close its indoor gym;
She posts as if to have no gym is such a heavy fate,
While I sit on my fraying couch, incredibly irate.

We Worked From Home.

Amidst the biking and the hiking and all the other things we endeavored to do to fight off monotony in the early months of the pandemic, I remember marveling at just how rapidly work life in America had changed completely.

The Hidden Joy of a Zoom Meeting

Suit on top, plus a dapper tie
That's what my colleagues can see;
Sweats on bottom – no one knows –
Happy, happy me!

Work From Home Secrets

Shhhh… don't tell my supervisor
That the tasks I've been assigned
Could easily be finished
In an hour or two combined.

She thinks they'll take the workday
And I like it best that way;
Oh and please don't tell her either
That I'm working from the beach today.

A Baby Shares My Office

I wrote this trying to step into the shoes of the millions of parents who somehow accomplished the superhuman feat of enduring a pandemic while parenting a child.

* * *

A baby shares my office now,
And he's frankly such a pain;
I've often had bad colleagues,
But this colleague is insane.

He cries extremely often,
Today, he pooped at work,
And when I ask for quiet
He acts like I'm the jerk.

I wish HR could help me,
To get this guy in line;
But they say that challenge falls to me
Since the baby in question is mine.

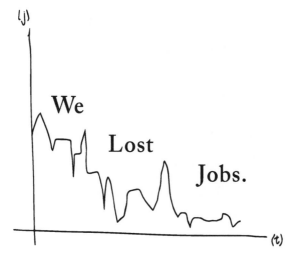

It was easy for me to forget in the early days of the pandemic that working from home – with all of its new dynamics and occasional headaches – was, in fact, a privilege.

Since so many of my own friends and family were lucky enough to continue in their jobs virtually, I sometimes needed to be reminded of just how many people didn't have that luxury.

There were of course the millions of essential workers, who had no choice but to risk their health by going into work. And then there were also the millions of others who had become unemployed. The numbers were staggering. And beneath the numbers was the reality that more and more Americans were being pushed to the financial brink.

Toward the end of November 2020, Feeding America, a hunger relief charity with a nationwide network of food banks, estimated that 1 in 6 Americans could end up facing hunger as a result of the pandemic. I remember reading that estimate in disbelief. In a nation as affluent as America, it was nothing less than a tragedy.

* * *

I had no way to truly imagine what it must have felt like to be hungry, or to be raising a family on a modest income and suddenly have that income disappear, or to have worked somewhere for decades only to have your job suddenly vanish. But still, I could witness elements of the devastation of the job loss. In particular, I could see the growing number of "For Lease" signs in the windows of newly empty stores and restaurants in my neighborhood. They served as constant reminders of all that had disappeared.

I wanted to write a poem reflecting on the precariousness of it all – the lost jobs and lost businesses – but it quickly became apparent that it wasn't my poem to write. So I wrote a different poem instead, offering up the one thing I thought I could provide in that moment – a little bit of levity and imagination.

I had recently read about the outbreaks of plague that had occurred when Shakespeare was living in London back in the 16th and 17th centuries. On more than one occasion the spreading of the plague caused the Globe Theatre, where Shakespeare's plays were performed, to close down. And so I decided to write a poem imagining what that temporary job loss might have felt like to Shakespeare himself.

I intended the poem, imagined in Shakespeare's voice, to be a creative reminder that 2020 was not the first time people had lost their jobs because of a devastating plague.

Knowing about previous pandemics wasn't going to make the real problems people were facing go away. But I hoped that perhaps recognizing that our moment in history had parallels in the past could help make the present feel just a little less cataclysmic.

Shakespeare in the Time of Plague

"My theater's been shuttered for months now
Thus I'm trying to contact the Queen,
For London's remained in the Red Zone for months,
Though our numbers should move us to Green,

My wife thinks that I should be worried,
That my theater career may be done;
I'm hearing the same from my mother-in-law
And from Hamnet, my only son,

They want me to start with some brainstorms
And to list other jobs I could do;
They think I would be a good miller,
Though I really don't think that that's true,

I tell them that things will get better,
They tell me that hope can't pay bills;
I tell them that this is my calling
They tell me I have 'other skills.'

I don't think that they understand me,
My dreams nor my love of the page;
They think that the world is a rat race;
I know that the world is a stage,

But it's far too much trouble to argue
So I choose to just smile and nod;
For it's best to avoid disagreement
With the rest of one's quarantine pod.

I bequeath to their ears what they yearn for
And I tell them I'll search for new work;
I give to them little objection,
My mouth bares no scowl nor smirk,

Yet, the moment they grant me seclusion
I dip my best quill in my ink,
And I rush to the land of ideas
And I dream and I write and I think,

They can live in the Kingdom of Worry,
But I've been and I'm not going back;
I reside in the Kingdom of Beauty
Where there's nothing I need that I lack,

Save a smidgeon of grace and of patience
For that patience will carry me through;
I'm not leaving this work I was made for
To mine own self I'll always be true."

By the fall of 2020, my girlfriend and I had moved into an apartment that was about a half-hour walk from Broadway, where the theaters remained just as shuttered as the Globe Theatre had occasionally been, centuries earlier.

Once in a while, I'd take that walk and wander through the theater-filled streets right by Times Square. Those streets had once felt to me like the center of the universe; now they were pervaded by an eerie quiet.

It made me sad, walking past the marquees for Hamilton, the Lion King and so many other treasured shows, knowing that the lights inside the theaters remained off, and that so many of the staff – the actors, the set designers, the ushers, the musicians – had certainly been furloughed or laid off.

What made me even sadder, though, was knowing that while so much of the country, like those who worked on Broadway, were suffering from the financial fallout of the pandemic, many of the richest Americans seemed to be getting even richer.

New Trustees in 2020

This poem is set at a virtual gala for one of the most prestigious art museums in the world, held in 2020.

* * *

"We are thrilled to introduce you
To our newest museum board
Comprised of the titans of industry
From companies that can't be ignored.

We are blessed to have Mr. Panetta,
A lead engineer from Zoom,
And Mrs. Lu, from Clorox,
Who is somewhere in this room,

We have Mrs. Jones from Campbell –
They've been selling lots of soup;
And Mr. Lamorella
From a mask production group,

We have Mrs. Kawasaki
An Amazon VP,
And last but not least, Mrs. Santos,
Whose company sells CBD.

* * *

It is clear that they're fit to help lead us
In our growth, they will each play a part;
And there's no other reason we chose them
Than because of their passion for art."

We Fell in Love with
Anthony Fauci.

With the job market and day-to-day life completely topsy-turvy, the one thing that felt consistently reliable to me was the steadying presence of Dr. Anthony Fauci, the most visible public health expert in America.

The Challenge of Leadership

When Moses was told to lead his people
He got a little bit grouchy;
Said G-d, "You think this job is hard –
Just look at Anthony Fauci's."

Man in a Lab Coat

There's a man in a lab coat on TV,
With glasses and silvery hair,
With a forthright voice and a tired look,
And a college professor's air.

He's speaking of testing and tracing
And the data on every vaccine,
And all I can think is I think I'm in love
With this angel on my screen.

I felt bad for Dr. Fauci sometimes. He made me think of a really wise middle school teacher who was fully aware that a big chunk of his class – in this case the American people – simply wasn't listening anymore.

Much of the noncompliance was clearly political. But I think at least a small part of the noncompliance, too, stemmed from the fact that people were just exhausted. They were exhausted because they missed so many of the joys of ordinary, pre-pandemic life. And I think they were exhausted, too, because of how exhausting living cooped-up lives can be.

We Drove Each Other Nuts. 💣

When I'd talk to friends who were living with others, most of them would acknowledge how grateful they were for the extra time they were getting with loved ones. But most of them, in the very same breath, would acknowledge that sometimes, sharing a living space with others literally 24/7 could be very, very hard.

27-Year-Old Back at Home

"Mommy – when is dinnertime?
Mommy – when is snack?
Mommy – can you wash my pants
And can you rub my back?

Mommy – where's my favorite shirt?
Mommy – where's my phone?
Mommy – can you leave my room
And let me be alone?

Mommy – why'd you touch my stuff?
And worse – without consent."
"Child – let me ask you this
Who here's paying rent?"

Could You Please Arrest My Husband?

Could you please arrest my husband
And send him to Alcatraz?
He's been getting on my nerves all week
And I don't like the beard he now has.

He's always leaving lights on
Which tends to make me frown,
The toilet seat is always up,
The WiFi's always down.

He never sweeps, unprompted,
It's like he's into dust,
And to his endless sports rants
I've long had to adjust.

His jokes are rarely new ones,
He has the loudest snore,
His socks, that never smell that good,
He leaves on our bedroom floor.

He loses things, then blames me,
He never makes the bed;
It's true – he does the dishes
But I'd love if he cooked instead.

Oh – and sometimes, when he "listens"
It's like he isn't there;
His mind seems on vacation
Like it's somewhere else – I swear –

So could you please arrest my husband
For his varied household crimes?
For the cluelessness and carelessness
He's shown too many times.

Though I guess, once you have got him,
Once you've put him in his cell,
Once you've given my dear partner
Just a tiny taste of hell

If you don't mind, Mr. Bailiff,
Let him out before too long,
Even if he's sometimes lazy,
Even if he's always wrong,

For the truth is, I will miss him
As his doting, loving wife;
Though he often drives me crazy,
He's the best thing in my life.

Noah and His Quarantine Pod

I suppose that Noah's family on the ark
Was the world's first quarantine pod.

I wonder what it was like for them
Without Netflix and Zoom,
Uber Eats and online shopping.

I wonder if Noah spent most of his days
Thinking lofty thoughts
About what he would do
When the flood finally ended,
Or if he spent more time
Asking his sons
To put their socks in the laundry basket.

I wonder if there were days when he lost his patience,
And nights when he went to sleep with an angry wife.

I wonder if by the end he was talking to the animals
Because he loved them,
Or simply because he had nothing left to say to anyone else.

I know they claim that Noah was a righteous man in his
generation,
But I think that even a righteous man can crack
When he's stuck inside
For weeks on end.

We Lifted Each Other

I imagine that almost no one who lived with others was completely immune to occasionally driving them crazy. There was no vaccine that could stop us from ever annoying our loved ones; nor was there a vaccine that could stop us from becoming annoyed by them.

But what interested me more than the ways people were getting on each other's nerves were the new ways people were finding to be kind and supportive to one another.

Though the pandemic brought out the worst in some people, it was clear that it brought out the best in others. To see that, all I had to do was look around, awed by all the people who, through their enormous kindness, were helping make pandemic life just a little bit easier for others to endure.

Somewhere in this City

Somewhere in this city
A nurse,
Hopped up on caffeine,
Shows up to work for the 7th day straight
For there are still lives waiting to be saved.

Somewhere in this city
A father tucks his daughter in
And tells her a bedtime story
Of unicorns and princesses and beautiful kingdoms far, far away
For there is still innocence
Worth holding on to.

Somewhere in this city,
A woman leaves a bag of groceries
On her elderly neighbor's doorstep
For there are still ways
To lend a hand.

Somewhere in this city
A boy paints a rainbow
And tapes it to his window
To proclaim to the world outside that brighter tomorrows are
on their way –
A landlord tells her tenant
To take an extra month to pay his bill –
A crisis counselor
Picks up the phone
To say to a young boy in need
"I am with you."

Somewhere in this city
Selflessness is born,
Each and every moment
In places where love still triumphs,
Even in darkness,
Even in pain.

The Ones Who Loved Us Through

Long after we forget
What it felt like to be walled in by the world
We will still remember
The people who loved us through,
Who lifted the world's weight above their heads,
Like superheroes holding up a falling building,
So that we could sneak out from beneath –
So that we could be safe,
When so much around us
Was crashing to the ground.

We Experienced

Loneliness.

The longer the pandemic went on, the more love and care it required to collectively keep lifting each other up. I don't know when exhaustion set in, but eventually it did.

For a majority of my friends and family, one of the biggest causes of that exhaustion was the loneliness of locked-down living. A few weeks apart from friends and family had been difficult but manageable. But months apart proved much, much harder.

Islands of Existence

In those lockdown days,
We made islands of our lives,
And lived on them,
Distant and untouched,
Far from the myriad ports at which we used to call.

It was peaceful sometimes on these islands we had no choice
but to make,
But it was lonely sometimes too,
Marooned from so many of those we love,
Waiting for the storm to pass,
For the waters to be safe
To take to the seas once more.

Loneliness and Solitude

How near the realms of loneliness and solitude are to each other,
And yet how far.

Passover for One

This poem was inspired by a conversation I had right before Passover in 2020 with an elderly man who is very dear to me. He was spending the holiday alone for the first time in his entire life. I wrote this poem thinking about him and all the other people who felt loneliness especially acutely whenever holidays would arrive.

* * *

He sits alone
In a small apartment,
All nine-and-a-half decades of him,
His first Passover
With no one on the other side of the table.

When he closes his eyes,
He can almost hear the voices of his children and grandchildren,
The hum of conversation,
The repetition of his son's old jokes,
The cracked but confident singing of the Four Questions.

But when his eyes open
It is only quiet;
There is no one here with him,
They belong to some other time,
To some other freedom
From a faraway past.

Empty Tables

Our tables once were often filled with guests,
Delicious feasts laid out, no effort spared;
To friends who'd come, we'd serve our very best,
And show them through our warmth how much we cared,
A home is always better when it's shared.
Our tables have been empty one whole year;
How much I wish my loved ones all were here.

We Lost Loved Ones.

It was never lost on me that I was among the lucky ones, spared the ultimate loneliness that coronavirus inflicted on millions of people: the loneliness of grief. It was a loneliness that threaded together men, women, and children all around the world, whose tables would never again be full.

It was inevitable that many people would die as a result of the pandemic. But in far too many places, the death tolls grew dramatically higher than they ever should have reached.

They Did Not Have to Die

In hospitals, the victims lie,
Their oxygen in short supply,
In sterile rooms, with dingy lights,
They toss and turn through sleepless nights,
With grit and fear, they grasp for breath
Endeavoring to outrun death;
They ache and sweat; they lie alone,
Uncomfortable, they writhe and moan
Amidst the sounds of anguished cries
And tearful FaceTime last goodbyes,
The nurses give their very best
The doctors fight with little rest
While leaders, miles away deflect,
The facts they stubbornly neglect,
They spin and hide, distract and blame
As if this all was just a game;
And then the victims pass away;
This did not have to be this way.

They Were Us

They were us.

Sons and daughters,
Grandfathers and grandmothers,
Husbands and wives,
Colleagues and classmates,
The fixtures in the landscapes of our lives,
And the ones who passed through rarely,
Like shooting stars,
Lighting up our worlds,
Even if only for a moment.

They were us.

They drove trucks and Teslas and old beat-up station wagons,
They loved the Yankees, the Patriots, the Bulls,
They hated the Yankees, the Patriots, the Bulls,
They lived in lavish apartments and underneath the scaffolding down the street,
They watched CNN and Fox News,
They went to church and to mosque and to synagogue,
And found the sacred too,
In the splendor of the great outdoors.

They were us.

Big spenders and worrywarts,
City folk and beach bums,
Homebodies and travelers,
Early-risers and night owls,
Dessert-orderers and kale eaters,
Friends who could make us hurt,
And ones who could help us heal.

WE LOST LOVED ONES

They were us.

They made music and art,
They ran marathons and planted flowers,
They gave us love and joy,
And sometimes headaches too.

They were us.

Selfish and kind,
Certain and confused,
Brave and afraid:
The ones we loved,
The ones we miss.

Remembering Their Names

500 years from now,
Children will open their textbooks
And they will read that beginning in 2020
A pandemic gripped the world
And took the lives of millions of people.

I wish they'd open their textbooks and read instead that in 2020
A pandemic gripped the world
And took the lives of Joseph Suriano,
A beloved teacher and coach,
And Dar'Yana Dyson who loved to dance,
And Valentina Blackhorse, who was only 28 years old,
Men and women and occasionally even children,
Who smiled and loved and laughed,
And looked no different than the millions the virus left behind.

I wish the textbooks of tomorrow were filled with photos of the victims
In their happiest moments,
Alongside scribbled notes of love from the family and friends who loved them,
For then the children of the future could see their world in ours,
Then those children could realize
That the past and the present are on the banks of the same river,
That yesterday can make today wise,
When we only heed its calls.

When I think about all of those lost, I think specifically about a woman named Pat, who passed away in November 2020.

She was one of the participants in the weekly writing workshop I taught to a group of senior citizens in Manhattan. In March, when the coronavirus struck, and our group started carrying out our sessions by conference call, Pat stopped joining us. It was only when one of the other participants told me that I learned why; she had tested positive for the coronavirus and was fighting the virus.

Though she technically survived coronavirus after contracting it in the first wave, as her daughter wrote "Survival is different from recovery in starkly obvious ways. In truth, she never really did recover. Her mind and body failed after Covid, continuously and visibly. Now that she is free, it has freed my mind of the recent image of her and allowed me to see Mom and remember her as she was."

I had always assumed that when the pandemic was controlled, I would get to see Pat again. I always imagined that she would be there whenever we got to resume our in-person sessions, walking with her walker to the door, a few minutes late as was her way, a smile lighting up her face. And yet, I won't. I will never see her smiling face again.

* * *

Pat was an amazing woman. She wrote beautifully and would regale the members of our workshop with stories from her past: childhood memories, school memories, travel memories. She would sometimes recite poems that she knew by heart. Once she brought in two marionettes that she had made a long time ago and passed them around; she had been an art teacher for years.

She had two cats and would talk about them all the time. Sometimes, as an activity, I would bring in uncaptioned cartoons for the group members to caption, and I always threw in cartoons that included cats, since I knew how much Pat loved them.

Pat laughed generously. She would sometimes insist that I join her for lunch after the workshop. I remember my joy the day I did. I found out after her death that she absolutely loved onion rings, and I'm fairly sure that was part of the meal she ate at that lunch.

She was kind and generous with compliments. She often let me know how much the workshop meant to her. And at the senior's residence, Pat always helped make new arrivals feel welcome with her warmth and her openness.

* * *

Day after day, I would look in the New York Times at the number of deaths from the day before, and whenever I'd try putting a real face on to the suffering that the coronavirus had unleashed, it was Pat's face that would come into my mind. It was remembering her smile and kindness that helped remind me that the growing number of deaths corresponded to real people, each with a story – and that every single death represented an incalculable loss.

2 562 739

There are numbers that are too large to understand.

Somewhere on the number line
Numbers get so big
That we forget
That big numbers
Are made of lots of little ones,
That 2 562 739 deaths
Started with one
And then another
And then another,
Over and over again.

Tell me the story of one man lost to this plague,
What he ate for breakfast,
What he called his grandson,
What photos he kept on his bedside table.

Tell me the story of one woman
Who this plague stole from this Earth,
What toothpaste she used,
What ice cream she preferred,
What nicknames her oldest friends still called her.

Tell me these stories,
For though there are numbers too large to understand,
One I can understand,
One can make me weep
And give me pause;
One can make me realize
Just how much has been lost
Invisible as it sometimes may be.

Note: The number in the title of this poem was the worldwide total number of coronavirus deaths reported by the Johns Hopkins Coronavirus Resource Center as of March 4, 2021.

We Were Flooded With Emotions.

As the number of deaths kept rising and the pandemic continued to stretch onward, my capacity to deal with the emotions of pandemic life definitely got weaker. In the earliest months of the pandemic, all the mindfulness practices I'd been cultivating were able to keep me largely grounded.

In those early pandemic months, like most people, I experienced a wide range of feelings. And yet, somehow, they did not overwhelm me; somehow I was able to hold them all, and remain mostly alright.

How Have You Been?

How have you been in this quarantine time?

Umm......
I have......

Sometimes been fearful and sometimes been cheerful and sometimes been weepy and sometimes been sleepy and sometimes been grateful and sometimes been hateful and sometimes been far-too-much stress on my plateful and sometimes been learning and sometimes been yearning and sometimes been awed at how much the world's turning and sometimes been asking when sports are returning and sometimes been lazy and sometimes been crazy and sometimes been judgy and sometimes been nudgy and sometimes been gloomy and sometimes been Zoomy and sometimes been happy and sometimes been snappy and sometimes been more than a little bit crappy and sometimes been grounded and sometimes astounded and sometimes completely and wholly confounded and sometimes reliant and sometimes defiant and sometimes expressive and sometimes obsessive and sometimes impatient and sometimes complacent and sometimes inspired and sometimes too tired and sometimes I'm somehow relaxed...

Does that answer the question you've asked?

By the pandemic's first winter, I was feeling down more often than I was feeling grounded. Article after article made it clear that tens of millions of other Americans were feeling down too. But that knowledge did little to ease my own feelings.

A Moping Day

Today I'm declaring a Moping Day,
A Take a Break from Coping Day,
A Snooze the Alarm Clock Freely Day,
A Teary, Touchy-Feely Day,
A Get Myself Some Flowers Day,
A Take At Least Two Showers Day,
An Ice Cream in My PJs Day,
A Buy What I Want at TJ's Day, *
A Mumbly Day,
A Grumbly Day,
A Grouchy Day,
A Couchy Day,
A Wish We Were Led by Fauci Day.

Today I'm declaring a Moping Day,
To be shared by everyone;
And I think I'll declare one every week
Until the pandemic is done.

*TJ's refers to Trader Joe's, the U.S. grocery store chain.

Joy and Sadness, Side by Side

You can climb to the top of the tallest peak
And marvel at the views,
Convinced you've found a paradise
Impossible to lose,

You can float on the waves of a dazzling sea
On a perfect summer day,
Assured the bliss you're cradled by
Will never go away,

But no matter how perfect the sprawling views,
No matter how blissful the sea,
No matter the lightness that meets your soul
Life gives no guarantee

That tomorrow the blessings of today
Will still reach out their hands;
That tomorrow the sea will still hold bliss
At the edge of the shoreline's sands,

For you cannot fence in happiness,
There is no magic door
To shut – and then be guaranteed
Good things forevermore,

As winter always touches spring,
As peace and war collide,
Life's sweetest gifts and harshest grief
Sometimes come side by side,

So it's best to learn to hold it all,
To welcome what arrives;
To juggle joy with sadness
In these ever-changing lives

WE WERE FLOODED WITH EMOTIONS

For life is gain but also loss,
It's pleasure mixed with pain;
It's sorrow mixed with great delight
It's sunshine mixed with rain.

We Looked For Hope.

Even in the midst of difficult moods, I tried my best to remain hopeful. It was hard – often near impossible – to stay optimistic when the world felt so heavy. But sometimes – even if only for a brief moment – I was able to muster optimism, finding inside of myself faith that better days were ahead.

This Too Shall Pass

This too shall pass,
This anxious time,
This storm that has no clear-cut end,

These stretching days
Of locked-down lives
And news too large to comprehend.

This trying time
Of constant change,
Of learning how to be apart,

These somber days
Of death and loss,
Of living with a heavy heart.

This vexing time
Of great unease,
Of things no longer guaranteed,

These homebound days
Of quarantine,
Cut off from hugs we sorely need.

This too shall pass,
This stressful time,
This fear that will not quickly leave,

I can't say when,
I can't say how,
But in this truth we must believe,

Let's walk this winding road as one
You lean on me, I'll lean on you;
There will be times when all feels lost
But one day, we shall make it through.

When All Feels Dark in this Big Wide World

When all feels dark in this big wide world
I sometimes think it's wise
To look to the stars way up above
That glint in the nighttime skies,

For the stars have seen eternities,
The rise and fall of kings;
The stars know even the wisest man
Can't know what tomorrow brings,

The stars have witnessed plague and war,
They've lived through flood and drought;
The stars have watched humanity
Contend with grief and doubt,

Yet still they shine, yet still they shine,
Like lanterns in the night;
Though darkness may not disappear
It's softened by the light.

To Sing Again

The cold disappears when it's greeted by spring,
The dark disappears when it's greeted by dawn;
A world hushed of music can still once more sing
As long as it knows that its music's not gone.

Tell Me of Days

Tell me of days when the sirens will cease,
When the poor and the pained and the worried will sleep;
Tell me of days when the lonely will heal,
When the comfort of love will embrace all who weep.

Tell me of days when the tired will rest,
When the lost will find hope through the power of grace;
When the Angel of Death will take leave of this world
And the Angel of Life will return in his place.

If the Redwoods Could Talk

If the redwoods could talk
I wonder what they'd say.

I saw one this past winter
That had lived through the Spanish Flu,
That had borne witness to the Civil War,
That had stood in its place for centuries
Watching the world go by.

I wonder if that tree is jaded now,
If it has seen too much suffering
To believe the world can be any other way.

If it had eyes,
I wonder if those eyes would be crying now,
Having seen the world zigzag
From one tragedy to the next,
From one misfortune to another,

Or if those eyes would notice instead
The world's zigzag
From hopelessness to hope,
From devastation to renewal,
From the edge of the abyss back to safer ground.

I wonder
If it would speak of the cold of winter,
Or of the flowers that grow in winter's wake,
If it would tell of trees splintered by lightning
Or of the ones that emerged in their place,
Reaching for the heavens,
Grateful
For the sun and the air.

The Rainbow

I am waiting for the rainbow
That comes when the storm subsides –
For the sky to smile and the sun to shine again,

I am waiting for the rainbow
That I know is on its way;
The only thing I do not know – is when.

We Found Reasons To Be Grateful.

Over the months and months of waiting for normalcy to come back, I learned a crucial lesson: to try to focus on what I was grateful for rather than on what I was lacking. For the days when it was hardest to count my blessings, I learned of a Yiddish proverb that felt especially apt for a pandemic moment: "If you cannot be grateful for what you have received," goes the proverb, "then be thankful for what you have been spared."

* * *

One of the biggest reasons for gratitude was the genuinely good news that vaccines had been approved and vaccination campaigns were underway; it was finally possible to see the light at the end of the tunnel. But the world was still in the tunnel, and so the passing days were still hard.

On those passing days, alongside my work, I tried to meditate and spend time outdoors to keep focused on all there was to appreciate. Some days I succeeded; other days I failed. But even when I failed, tomorrow was always waiting for me – another chance to find brightness in a much-too-dark world.

All That's Still Here

I wanted to ask G-d about the dead and the dying,
But then I saw a swaying tree,
And I listened to the gentleness of its rustling leaves,
And a bird chirped,
And the sun shone through,
And a boy on his bike rode by smiling from ear to ear,
And for a precious moment
I did not want to ask about all that had been lost,
But only to notice
All that was somehow
Still here.

A Thank-You Note to Today

One day I'd like to slow the world down enough
To sit and make a list
Of all the things I'm grateful for.

Love,
And sleep-ins,
And showers with perfect water pressure,
And enduring friendships,
And mesmerizing books,
And all-you-can-eat buffets,
And perceptive compliments,
And Pixar films,
And the authenticity of people who do not try to be anyone but
themselves.

One day I'd like to silence the voice
That asks if there are better tomorrows I've yet to find,
One day I'd like to do nothing but scribble out
A thank-you note
To today

To beauty,
And music,
And well-told stories,
And unexpected kindness,
And the patience of good teachers
And moments of inner peace
When the mind's monologue completely fades away.

One day I'd like to be nowhere but where I am
To visit neither the future nor the past
To make snow angels in today
To catalog the blessings of this wondrous world.

Majestic sunsets,
And matzah ball soup
And art that has no pretense

WE FOUND REASONS TO BE GRATEFUL

And good back tickles
And board game nights
And the weather on those rare days that it's just right;
The list goes on and on.

This world is a treasure chest
But most of us never find it;
Most of us live ever-wanting lives
Constantly searching
For riches we already possess.

Morning Prayer

When I was a boy
We used to start the school day with prayer,
Giving thanks
For our eyes reopening,
Our bodies reawakening,
Our breath continuing to keep us alive.

It felt confusing
Saying thank you,
For what it seemed would be ours forever;
Only now do I realize,
We were giving thanks for miracles;
Only now do I realize
We were learning how not to forget
The gift of a brand-new day.

Scattering Thanks

I remember watching a little cousin once,
Who was a flower girl at a wedding,
Walk down the aisle,
Scattering flowers every which way,
The widest smile
Lighting up her little face.

I want to scatter thanks
The way she scattered those flowers,
With a blissful abandon.

I want to give away every last ounce of gratitude
So that eventually I am left with nothing but the joy that comes
in its place,
So that when I get down the aisle of a life fully lived,
I am holding only the knowledge
That love is never best saved
For another day.

We Tried To Be Kind To Ourselves.

Near the end of the winter, at the very beginning of March 2021, I remember confronting a particularly strong sensation of pandemic fatigue. Almost a full year had passed since the world had changed so dramatically, and still it was unclear what the future was going to bring.

* * *

On one of those early March 2021 days, I had a phone conversation with a friend that I can still recall. I told him how exhausted I was by everything, almost disappointed with myself.

"It's a pandemic," he responded laughing, and then reminded me, as many others had as well, to be kind and gentle to myself.

It was advice I'd given to others countless times throughout the year – but still, it was remarkably hard to follow myself.

And yet it was the advice that I, and millions of others, needed most. To be patient. To be loving and understanding with ourselves. In short, to remember that these days were among the hardest we'd hopefully ever live through, and that it was okay if we did not find beauty or a silver lining in each and every one of them; that simply making it through was more than enough.

We Are Enough

We are enough on our darkest days
When the mind feels like it can't go on,

We are enough on our longest nights
When we lie awake awaiting dawn.

We are enough at our most unwell,
At our most afraid and our most confused,

We are enough when our hearts are pained
And our spirits ache and our souls are bruised.

We are enough when we feel we're not
When we're lost and don't know what to do,

We are enough and we'll always be;
Imagine if we only knew.

Give Yourself Time to Feel

Give yourself time to be sad.

Give yourself time to be bored,
And lonely,
And confused,
And impatient,
And annoyed by your little brother
Who can't seem to understand
What privacy means.

Give yourself time
To be selfish,
And needy,
And tired,
And wishing you were somewhere
Other than where you are.

Give yourself time
To break down,
To want the things you cannot have,
To fear the things you do not know,
To stare at the wall
Shell-shocked by the shapelessness
Of now.

Give yourself time
Every single day,
Alongside the yoga classes,
And the Zoom calls,
The meetings and the meditations,
To feel all that floods your soul –
That which you cherish
And that which you wish you could chase away.

There are times for self-improvement,
But there are times for self-compassion too;
This is a time for the latter,
This is a time for gifting yourself every little kindness that you
can.

We yearn for tenderness from others,
This is the time
To give it
To yourself.

The Bumpiness of Being Human

We try so hard
To tinker our lives towards perfection,
As if they were cars in need of constant upgrade,
As if one more podcast or Pilates class,
Might suddenly melt away,
The bumpiness of being human.

Day by day,
We try to chip away at our flaws
Only to realize that these lives of ours will always be blemished,
That they can be polished endlessly and still they could be polished more,
That to chase perfection is to live blindfolded
To the myriad moments that are perfect enough;
To the times when we have already arrived to where we need to be,
And yet still believe
There are miles left to go.

Weather Patterns of the Mind

If I learned to think of my moods as the weather
Perhaps I would blame myself for them less,
Perhaps I would remember that try as you might
You cannot stop the rain
Or chase away the clouds,
Sometimes all you can do,
Is remember the forecast is always changing,
Is know that you will remain
Long after the fog has lifted
And the sun shines down again.

To the Ones Whose Minds Are Hurting

To the ones whose minds are hurting
In a world that's disconcerting,
And the ones whose days too often feel like night;

To the ones besieged by worry
For the future's grown so blurry
They no longer trust that things will be alright.

To the ones who yearn for healing,
But still cannot shed the feeling
That there's only disappointment up ahead;

To the ones weighed down by sorrows,
With no faith in their tomorrows,
And the ones who some days can't get out of bed.

To the lonely and the aching,
To the ones whose hearts are breaking
Not just once – but every single day anew;

To the fragile and the battered,
To the ones whose dreams feel shattered,
And the ones afraid they may not make it through:

When it's heaviest – this living –
When the world feels unforgiving,
When the mountain that you climb feels far too tall,

When you see the paths that greet you,
And it seems they will defeat you,
And you never in your life have felt so small,

Take a breath and then another,
Put one foot before the other,
Try to meet this heavy moment day by day;

WE TRIED TO BE KIND TO OURSELVES

Through the burdens that you're juggling
Keep on moving, keep on struggling;
And I promise – one day things will be okay.

We Begin To Look Forward.

It's the middle of March 2021 now as I finish writing this book. Spring is almost here. The weather is warming and winter seems to be finally loosening its grip. There's hope that the pandemic is doing the same. I sense more possibility in the air, even if it's a possibility mixed with fatigue and loss.

* * *

Early in the pandemic, I remember a friend wondering aloud on a Zoom call how the world would know when the pandemic was over. What would it mean, he had wondered, for a global plague to be done?

There would be no bell, my friend had said to me back then, to suddenly announce the closing of this chapter in our lives. The pandemic's ending, he had imagined at the time, would likely be far more confusing.

* * *

My friend's comments feel especially resonant to me now in this strange transition period it seems the world is in. It feels like we've finally arrived at the beginning of the pandemic's end and yet it's unclear if that's just a feeling or reality.

A vaccination campaign marches forward in America with an ever-accelerating target date for vaccines to be available to all American adults. Yet still, case numbers remain high; still, deaths number well above a thousand almost every day; still, new variants are spreading that threaten to undo some of the progress of vaccinations.

More local to my own life, a sense of changing times has arrived in New York City, as restaurants and movie theaters reopen, and I notice my vaccinated friends and acquaintances begin to change their behaviors. And yet my day-to-day remains largely the same as it has been this past year – still almost entirely at home, in the same quarantine routines I've been living with for one whole year now. It's a confusing moment.

In this confusion, I've been reflecting on the lessons I've learned from this first year of pandemic living. I've learned about human resilience and endurance. I've learned about loss and fragility and the unpredictable nature of life. I've learned about loneliness and courage, creativity and self-compassion, hope and healing. And I've learned that even in a collective moment of tumult and pain, it is still possible to grow and change for the better; difficult times can make us bitter and cynical, but they can also enlarge our spirits and our understandings of ourselves.

* * *

As I look back on these lessons I've learned, for the first time in more than a year I'm simultaneously starting to look forward. It's a strange feeling, after living for so long in what has felt like a perpetual present, to allow oneself to start thinking further ahead. A few weeks ago, I got a save-the-date for a friend's small wedding he's hoping to celebrate about six months from now and I noticed as I put it in my calendar that it didn't seem like completely wishful thinking. That same week, I chatted with a friend from college who lives abroad about visiting him – a reunion we had hoped to make happen before the pandemic – and the idea that it might be possible within the next year didn't seem completely out of the question. I've started to see beyond tomorrow again, and it's exciting and liberating.

But it's also scary. It's scary because this past year for me has been a cocoon. It has sometimes been an anxiety-filled cocoon and it has sometimes been a claustrophobic cocoon and it has sometimes been a terribly dark cocoon. But still it has been a cocoon and there's a certain coziness and safety to a cocoon.

Now comes the beginning of a moment of transition, and transitions – even when they're welcome – are scary. We get comfortable with what we know, and over this past year what I've come to know is this strange pandemic life to the point where it's the before times that feel unfamiliar. I'm excited to return to those before times, but I'm nervous too about having to readjust to an opening-up world: having to relearn what I want out of my in-person social life, reassess what communities I hope to be a part of, reconsider how to balance travel with home, reintegrate all the good things I've missed into my life without overstuffing it.

And so, my aim is to transition lightly, gently, self-compassionately. As I do, I have only one hope – which is to carry with me the lessons from this still ongoing pandemic time, and to let them shape me and guide me. I know there will be a temptation to quickly push these lessons away – to latch on to the false belief that holding on to a difficult past and its wisdom is somehow incompatible with fully embracing the post-pandemic present when it arrives. But I believe strongly that when this pandemic truly is over, holding on to its memories for the sake of heeding its lessons is what, in fact, will ensure that it does not cast a shadow over our present, but instead shines a light.

Tragedy can never be fully undone. This past year has been a tragedy and no amount of historical revisionism can change that. As I write this final paragraph, America has lost well over 500 000 lives to the coronavirus and the world has lost close to 3 million; those lives are never coming back. But when we learn from tragedy, at least it can be partially redeemed. At least it can make us wiser and kinder and more openhearted. At least then, all that we have lost in this year like none before will not have been lost completely in vain.

Acknowledgements

There are so many people to thank who have helped me bring this book to publication.

To everyone who provided me edits, thanks for your generosity and your valuable feedback. A special thanks to Abby Klionsky and Julie Meyer – your keen editing skills were tremendously useful in helping turn this book into the best version of itself.

To Tess Lockey, thanks for making a fantastic cover and for being so easy to work with.

To Shane Ah-Siong, thanks for your beautiful interior illustrations and design.

To the hundreds of people on my Poem of the Week email list, thanks for being a part of my writing journey. A writer is nothing without readers, and it's been your readership each and every week of the pandemic that has motivated me to keep putting my ideas into poetry during these challenging, uncertain times.

To the authors and screenwriters whose books, movies, and TV shows have kept me entertained throughout these long homebound months, thanks for your words and for the worlds they've created.

To my wonderful friends, thanks for the enormous joy you bring to my life.

To Bubby and Grandma, thanks for being so special to me; I love you both dearly. I wish Zaidy and Grandpa were alive to read this book.

To Jordy, thanks for the sushi lunch and for the online Settlers games.

To Josh, thanks for the almost nightly video chats that have been one of the highlights of my pandemic experience, and for the almost weekly Chinese food you bought me that never failed to bring a huge smile to my face.

To my Dad, thanks for always encouraging my ideas and my work, and for modeling for me how to deal with some of the unexpected challenges of the pandemic with grace and patience.

To my Mom, thanks for being such an amazing mother and for being such a spectacular cheerleader of my work. I know you'd do anything for me.

And to Pavla, thanks for your inexhaustible love and compassion in these crazy, unprecedented months. How lucky I am to be weathering this pandemic with you.

Made in the USA
Columbia, SC
03 June 2021